Waiting
at
Bloomsbury Park

Casey Bailey

Talai

Thank you for your support!
Your work with young people in the
arts is inspiring, and i'm glad you
still support the old guys. :)

x

C.B.

Waiting at Bloomsbury Park
© Casey Bailey, 2017

Artwork: Kerri Bailey
Edited by Amerah Saleh and Paul Bell-Stoddart

First Published in the UK in 2017
by Big White Shed, Nottingham
Printed in the EU by Booksfactory

www.bigwhiteshed.co.uk
www.baileysrapandpoetry.com

from Nechells to the world

This book is dedicated to the memory of
Christine Bailey.

More than a woman, more than a mother,
more than we deserved.

Waiting at Bloomsbury Park

Marbles

Green over orange, over green.
The kids play marbles here, and
as the sun reaches down to kiss
the smooth, curved glass
I see the colours somersault.

Tower blocks rise above them.
Vertical villages
casting shadows on those inside and out,
patches on green grass and orange bricks.

Kids roll marbles, police roll by,
all fun and games until it isn't.
Marbles bang like gun shots,
smashed glass, clash like gang members.

This is where they learn
to handle victory and defeat.
Some feel like they'll never win.
They play for keeps here, and they always will.

Flipping Coins

We've been flipping coins to make decisions,
following friends that we don't trust,
claiming that we're on a mission,
convincing ourselves what we do is just.

I've been flipping coins to make my mind up,
you've been finding lies that suit your truth,
I'm trying to work out why I signed up,
while you just blame it on your youth.

They'll be flipping coins that shape our future,
we'll be fighting, but won't know what for,
they'll decide what we want as consumers,
we'll convince ourselves we want more.

Coins flip, coins land, heads or tails.
Understand, either way, we fail.

Fresh Litter

Sun shining doesn't make it feel any less gloomy.
Shadows cast by tower blocks cannot hide the mess.
I see fresh litter to my left and right, it's inescapable.

Not crushed, not muddied, not even fully used.
Fresh like coffee
straight from the filter, steaming and unsullied.
No milk, no sugar, no cream, no sweetener.
Fresh.

This Coke can
probably holds the last drops of the beverage,
the dregs we used to call them;
the spit backs.
Its reds and whites are more vibrant than stop signs,
but nobody is gonna stop for it,
nobody is gonna pause when they see it,
who else sees it anyway,
who else even cares, do I?
Fresh litter doesn't become the time-worn kind
over time, or gracefully.
If you've never seen a kid stamp on a Coke can,
you've never seen true destruction for distraction.

Wind whistles by,
whispering words I can't capture,
saying enough to take the fresh Coke can to sit
with the old litter.
Sometimes this is how it happens.
We have a saying where I'm from,
if you lie down with dogs you get fleas.
Bright red Coke cans don't belong
with flattened cigarette packets,
rolled on by bike wheels,
picked up by broken men
and discarded again.

I don't know what the wind whispered.
Bright red Coke cans don't belong here.

Sometimes;
nowhere near often enough,
somebody sees the beauty in fresh litter,
they take it home,
and they love it like nobody else ever could.
Sometimes.

Haunted

Summer days haunt me.
Summer days with you haunt me.

I am haunted by train rides from Birmingham to Liverpool.
We had no ticket, no fear, just two virgins on one Virgin.
I am haunted by house parties in posh towns, where two
ghetto boys stand out like Birmingham building site bricks
at the Barton-on-Sea pebble beach.

I am haunted by laughter, sun tans on already tanned skin,
energy drinks laid heavily on already energetic hearts,
inappropriate comments passed
in the presence of police officers,
I'm haunted by fresh haircuts in stale barbershops.

I dream of lavender blooming,
attracting honey bees
like ice cream vans
attracted us on summer days.
Dreams turn to nightmares,
lavender kicked to tatters
by absent minded boys like us,
on summer days like these.

I am haunted by summer days.
I am haunted by summer days with you.

Laser Pens

We used to dance like laser pens.
Laser pens on classroom ceilings,
laser pens in 5th period chemistry
hiding when people looked in our direction.

We used to dance like laser pens.
Laser pens on midnight tower blocks;
you could reach me from further away
than eyes could see, further than the lasers.

We used to dance like laser pens,
like torches, or spot lights on a stage,
like lyrics flowing through the verse,
like the singer with the microphone.

We used to dance like laser pens
until you flickered, like an eye flutter,
camera shutter; blink and you miss it.
You flickered, you faded, you fizzled.

We danced like children in puddles,
like dogs when fireworks bark outside.
Now I dance alone. I dance for you,
like a laser pen looking for another.

Wax

He told me he would fly to the sun one day.
He would push from these
city streets,
these gritty streets,
he would push and fly
higher than the rockets that NASA send,
he would fly to the sun one day.

I told him that's what Icarus said.
Brave boy with feathered wings,
held together with wax. Brave boy
with bigger dreams than he'd ever seen.
I told him that's what Icarus said.

He told me he would fly to the sun
he would fly higher than
Thames Tower
Medway Tower
Severn Tower
than those towers
stacked one on top of the other
even if the crackheads that live in those towers
the police that raid the flats of the crackheads
that live in those towers
tried to stop him
he would make it.

I can't help but smile at the way he holds
police and crackheads
with the same level of disdain;
I know he hates
the police more,
know he's more scared
of becoming the crackheads.
He told me he would fly to the sun.

I told him that's what Icarus said.
Brave boy with feathered wings,
held together with wax. Brave boy
ready to battle, stronger and harder

ready to defy all the advice given, ready to fly.
I told him that's what Icarus said.

He looked me in the eyes,
surprised I gave him so little credit.
He said *fam, what kind of idiot holds their dreams together with wax*
when their dreams involve the sun?
I listen and I laugh.
We laugh.

I laugh because everyone I know
would tell me he doesn't get it,
and he would tell them that they don't get it,
and I'm starting to think Icarus didn't get it.

This brave boy with wings held together
by hope, desperate to escape a labyrinth
that his father created for him. Desperate
but determined to live, to rise, to fly.

I have never seen anyone stuck so long
in a nightmare and still manage to hold
so strong to their dreams. For a second
maybe half, I believed him.

Silence on the Dance Floor

We are gladiators in the arena,
blood flying like cold, judgemental looks
in PE changing rooms and school canteens.
We are dancers on lonely dance floors,
failing to hear any of the music playing,
feeling every beat pulsing from our hearts.

They scream words that we can't hear,
even if we stop, stand still, silently still,
noise does not exist where we are now.

We dance on silent dance floors that they
made for us, on silent dance floors they led us to,
on silent dance floors, for them.

We never chose this, and we know this,
but heaven help us if we show this.

This is our arranged marriage, after our
slave carriage, with insane savages clamouring.
They scream a type of silence that breaks
only when we do, or at least one of us.

We don't even want to win,
we just want to hear the music pierce this silence again.

When He Told You

When he told you that nobody else would love you,
he lied.
When he told you he would never lie to you,
he lied.
When he told you he didn't know why she called,
he lied.
When he told you he didn't know that his phone rang,
he lied.

When he told you that you were strong,
and he sounded surprised,
he was exposing you to how little he thinks of you,
how much he thinks of himself.

When he told you that you should leave if
you don't trust him, that wasn't because
he thought that you'd trust him,
that wasn't because he wanted you to leave.
He didn't believe you could do it.

When he told you he didn't need you
you should have tested him.
When he told you he was gonna leave you
you should have let him.
When he told you he didn't love you
you should have listened.
When he told you to find someone better

you should have.

Canals

We are canals.
We are stagnant,
still, stuck and stale.

We are canals.
No flow, no go.
No destination.

We are canals.
They wouldn't be
there if it weren't
for what we are,
we wouldn't
be where we are
if it wasn't
for who they are.

But who wants to
be where we are?

We are canals.
We are dirt, grit,
rubbish and spit.

We are canals.
We are unsafe,
never trusted.

We are canals.
We are blackness,
abandonment,
needed no more.
Still here to
hear stillness,
deep but shallow.
Always changing,
never moving.

But who wants to
be where we are?

We are canals.
We are dirt, grit,
still, stuck and stale.

We are canals.
No flow, no go.
Never trusted.

Delivery

He tapes his love letters to bricks
throws them through windows
and waits for responses that never come.

Love letters littered with literary devices
turning scriptures into pictures
that can be seen and smelled, heard and felt.
He weaves sensational tapestries of love
and he can't believe they are ignored.

He is floored, when his manifesto
that is branded into human flesh
does not earn him the votes he requires.
How are people uninspired by the words
he burns them with?

He types criticism onto bullets.
Feedback fired, piercing hearts
and penetrating minds. Bullet points;
points of bullets don't land softly.

He taped his love letters to bricks
threw them through windows
and waited for responses that never came.

This morning he found a brick in
the middle of his living room,
heart shaped Post-it note attached.
*Sometimes it's not about what you
say, it's about how you say it.*

Skater Girl

I know a girl who skates.
She rollerblades on a knife edge
as unbalanced as anyone I ever met.
I feel fear bubbling in my stomach.
I do not fear that she will cut herself if she falls,
we both know she does that already.

Red ladder ripped into her arm;
her personal physical feedback forum.
Red ladders on her arm,
serpents in her life.
This is no game.

She tells me she won't say that vile, hated word,
so she just says, he vio-lat-ed her.
We both know what she means,
we both know how this works.

She talks, I listen.
She talks, I listen.
She cries, she screams, I listen.
Sometimes I talk. Sometimes she listens.
Sometimes I talk so she doesn't have to listen.

I'm not here to tell her things she doesn't know.
I'm here to show her things she has always known.
She is broken, but never beyond repair.

I know a girl who skates. She
rollerblades on a knife edge.

Gravestone

Sit with me and read your gravestone.
Don't cry, you're not dead yet, we are
flashing forward from here to there;
not because you want it, because you need it.

Your gravestone sums you up
in a pithy little quote.
It will never do you justice
but it will never do you harm.

Your gravestone will make you
the possession of your loved ones,
those who will hold you in their hearts,
long after they can hold you in their arms.

You will be daughter,
sister, wife, mother.

You will be theirs forever,
and they will be yours.

Your gravestone won't mention
the time you screamed at your son,
it won't mention the time you
kicked your brother after he told
your first boyfriend that you
practised kissing with your hand.

Your gravestone will turn you
into an ethereal, perfect creature.
This is not because your loved ones lie,
this is the truth of you in their hearts.

You are magical, not because you are gone,
because of all you were when they had you.
So go; love and live like
they will say you did,
forgive yourself when
you get it wrong.
They will.

Obsessing and Waiting

I remember how you obsessed over
little things, little to me, big to you.

You had this gap in the middle of your chest.
A chasm between two perfectly formed pecs,
and you obsessed about it.

You asked me what I thought of your outfits.
You knew damn well that I have no fashion sense,
but you waited, cautiously on that opinion.

You obsessed like a child in the mirror.
A child who felt like his mother didn't love him,
obsessing over why.
Cold gaze blowing winter snow across a desert
where self-esteem once lived.
You obsessed.

You waited like a boy at the window,
a boy waiting for his dad to come,
a boy waiting for his dad to love him.
You waited in darkness, even at noon
during the summer, darkness, and you waited.

Now I obsess. I obsess over the sad fact that you were that boy,
I ask myself if your obsession with little things
was just a distraction from the big things,
that you were never really ready to face.

Now I sit with no gap in my chest, but a canyon in my heart.
I obsess over whether I supported you enough.
I wait for you to come and reassure me.
You won't. So, I obsess, and I wait.

Dreams and Nightmares

Have you ever looked at the sky
and panning from left to right,
seen the most dark and temperamental
clouds blending into the most
beautiful and magical red hues?

I have seen the sky hold the most
vicious nightmares
and wondrous dreams
in the palm of its hand.

Sometimes I wonder if nature gives
us omens in the form of physical
metaphors. Sometimes I wonder if
I overthink. Battle in my mind, battle
in the sky; dreams and nightmares.

I have cried tears whilst ecstatic, not
tears of joy, tears of pain, for those
lost too soon to experience this magic.

I have laughed whilst broken; far
too busy remembering friendships,
laughing about experiences, to even
acknowledge the chasm that has
been left, by the friends I have lost.

I have been weighed down under the
shadow of pessimistic clouds, yet
simultaneously illuminated by the
radiance of a night sky that glows.

I know the skies do not hold dreams
or nightmares, but when I look to them,
I can't help but stop and think of you.

Road to Ruin

He's burned down the village again!

They hadn't even finished rebuilding
it this time; walls half-formed, houses
with no roof, no longer walls, or houses.

Bricks and mortar destroyed. Of course
they're a loss, but not the worst casualty
of this fire. He's set fire to hope, left
love lying lifeless, wrecking balls through
order and structure, hammer blows
through the fibres of all that is right!

Pete Doherty said,
I have a very bad relationship with the future,
we don't get on. We just ignore each other.
Some see him as a messianic messenger,
some maniacal madman, but his
relevance of experience, and eloquence of
expression, is undeniable and inescapable.

He has burned down the village again!

I tell this story to a boy, making it clear
to him that this isn't like Pompeii, this
is destruction at the hand of man, this
is avoidable. I so carefully communicate
the moral of this story, but to hide from
the boy that there is no village, just a
man, setting fires. A man I know he
will see, but truly hope he won't be.

The First Girl I Ever Kissed

The first girl I ever kissed
probably regrets it as
much as she regrets the last
man that she kissed. Enough
to reflect but not enough
to refrain when she's put
in the same position again.

It's not the way I clumsily
bashed her teeth with mine, more
the way I clumsily fumbled
her hopes and wishes
for this special moment.

Her eyes still closed as I ran.
It was a kiss goodbye
and I didn't want to miss my bus.

I don't regret many things,
but I wish I had missed
that bus, and stopped to tell her
how unimportant it was.

Broken Crown, Broken Kingdom

I'm sitting on the carriage statue, just outside Bloomsbury Park.
I found out since that it is a monument to the Lanchester Car
but to the kids of Nechells it was always The Carriage.

I'm sitting in the driver seat, and I feel like the King of Nechells.
In case you don't know; Nechells is a dump!
But we are like pigs
we have learned to love the grime that we live in.
We roll in it, rest in it, sleep in it.
We get mad when we are not stuck here in this muck.

From my throne I can rotate, and see 360 degree
panoramic views of my kingdom.
At least ten tower blocks visible from here,
two drunk men at 11 o'clock
a Staffordshire Bull Terrier at 12;
off the lead, on the rampage.

I see kings of the past, looking neither royal nor regal.
I see princes and princesses
whose only aim, desire and dream
is to sit on this throne.

I still don't know when or how it happened
but driven by motivation and determination
seeping from my pores, The Carriage took flight
and carried me here. I am no longer the king
but I finally realise, that pigs in muck
aren't as happy as they make out.

Sometimes I walk, drive or run past that carriage.
I give it a little nod.
When young kings and queens, rest upon its thrones
I whisper, *save them*.

I Hear You

I hear you.
When the morning sky hears the sun creaking,
climbing from just beyond the blazing horizon,
I hear you.

I see you.
When a newborn sees light for the first time,
piercing like needles through the reality that once was,
I revel in the marvel of you, crying tears of freedom, free,
as they are from the womb, I find freedom within your arms.
I see you.

I smell you.
When the beaches smell the coming of the tide, audible
and auspicious, waves rolling with a purpose, a destination.
I smell you.

I taste you.
When the night sky tastes stardust;
the finest sugar sprinkled across its palate,
sweeter than everything but you.
I taste you.

I feel you.
When the clouds feel the rumble of thunder,
when vibrations carry threats, and promises without words.
I feel you.

I love you.
When similes and metaphors paint broken pictures,
when personification and pathetic fallacy can no longer
do reality justice, I love you; plain, simple, without apology
or reservation.
I love you.

I Will Be Fine

I cried and she held my head.
She told me it was fine. It wasn't.

It wasn't fine, but I was;
I always would be
as long as she was there to hold my head.
I would be fine.

When I scraped my knee
waterfall of blood streaming
down my shin, antiseptic wipe
sending shockwaves through
my system, I was fine.
She held my head and I was fine.

When metal blades broke
my skin, when plastic friends
broke my trust, and death
broke my heart, I was fine.
She was there and I was fine.

I carried my best friend's coffin
tears like tsunami waves, unrelenting.
He chose suicide and I had to live with it.
I struggle to manage the idea that anything
could be harder than trying to cope with losing him.
It must have been harder for him. He wasn't fine
but she was, so I knew I would be.

Now she's gone. I am a throne
without a queen, a queen
without her crown, a heart
without its beat. I am broken.

This brain carries memories
more precious than any jewel
this heart is hallmarked with love;
this is unbreakable.

While I am here, her stories
will live in my mind, her spirit
will dance forever in my heart.

I will be fine.
Sometimes I won't even want to be,
but I will be fine.

Oliver Twist

Often people ask me why I say I'm living the dream,
and I can't help but feel that if they didn't understand
before they asked,
then they won't understand after I answer,
but I tell them anyway.

How can I ask more of life
when there are wars raging around this world
where the ones most likely to die
are the ones least likely to gain?

From Syria to Yemen.
Conflicts that conspire to conscript children,
callously causing the catastrophic cessation of childhood,
like a caesarean section after the fact.
Not cut from mother's womb, but ripped from mother's arms,
taking her heartbeat with them,
like some subconscious remnant of an umbilical cord
refusing to let go.

How does a mother even motivate herself to survive,
knowing only too well, that her son will be killed
and never return, or kill another,
to return as dead emotionally as his adversaries are physically?
How does she even know which one to pray for?
Which one would be the kinder fate?

How can I ask more of life
when there are wars raging around this world
where the ones most likely to die
are the ones least likely to gain,
Somalia to Sudan, Palestine to Ukraine?
How can I ask more of life?

As a boy I sat on the same pendulum that I rest upon now
where the view is always a benchmark for comparison.
It's strange how much the view has changed
considering I swing from the same pivot point as I did then.

I used to talk of silver spoons, misfortune and injustice,
I would compare my life with those whose material belongings
held more 'value' than my own.
A young Oliver Twist, I begged for more.
It's funny how we look to those who have plenty
when we beg for more.
Is it to save ourselves from the shame
of looking to those who have none?
How dare I beg for more
knowing there are people who merely beg for some?
Worse still, there are people who beg only for less.
Less war, less pain, less heartache.
Please sir, can we just have less!

To deal with a fear of heights, they say never look down.
This is fine advice for a climber; climbing mountains
or climbing the social and financial ladders
that dominate the minds of many.
Don't look down.
But if you wish to appreciate the height at which you stand,
if you wish to appreciate the beauty of the view,
if wish to understand the devastation of the fall,
at some point you must look down.

How can I ask more of life
when looking up shows me a summit
that it is a mere whisper away,
and looking down shows me clouds,
so high am I above the ground
that I do not see the depths of the valley.

I can barely make out the base camp from which I am climbing,
a base camp that most wouldn't dream of reaching.
I didn't climb there,
I was born there,
saved by life from the calluses of the journey.

How can I ask more of life
when there are wars raging around this world
where the ones most likely to die
are the ones least likely to gain?

Dear Birmingham

Dear Birmingham. That doesn't even sound right,
Yo Brum, that's the kind of thing that I would write.
That's not because you're not dear to me, or always here for me,
but I have heard your bark and more than once I felt your bite.
So how you keeping? Still having trouble with your sleeping?
When I think of you, I think about the long extended evenings,
nights that turn to mornings,
young brothers snatched from good mothers,
I think about the nights that we spent mourning.
Think of Charlene Ellis and Letisha Shakespeare,
their family pain at the shame knowing that they ain't here.

It's crazy, how quick mom or dad can lose a baby,
Brum I love you, but at times I truly feel that you've betrayed me.
Brum I love you, I know I seem focused on your flaws,
but I have seen so many die claiming postcodes that are yours.
I've no intention to draw attention to funerals I've attended,
just to mention your malfunctions so one day they may be mended.

Sometimes I think you're so sweet, but you use that to distract me.
Man I never thought that Cadbury would turn out to be so Krafty,
surely we could have fought for whole nuts,
Brum, aren't we tough enough?
Instead we showed no nuts, and decided we should button up.
I don't wanna sound like a complainer, or rant like a moaner,
and I realise it's been a long time since Rover,
but the drama and the rubble since they built the last bubble,
means this will be a long bridge for those people to get over.

Brum I love you,
I know this isn't clear from my statements,
but as a man,
you didn't live up to my boyhood expectations,
still if they told me to let go,
I'd have to tell them No, No, No,
like Amy offered rehabilitation.
Home of my relations, birthplace of my dreams,
fuelling my motivation stronger than kerosene.
They call it the second city,
but whenever I spend a second out the city,

I know there's nowhere better I could be.
Proud Birmingham son; married one of your daughters,
met her in Kings Norton, bought the ring in Jewellery Quarter,
now I use her like an anchor, my connection to Brum,
like the anchor hallmark that they're pressing in Brum.
Home of the innovators, focused on solutions,
like Matthew Boulton leading industrial revolutions.
It's easy to have a vision, anybody can dream,
it's different to reach goals, burn coal, make steam.

You ain't seen Brum if you haven't seen the tower blocks,
and tried to define where the clouds start and the towers stop.
You ain't heard Brum, unless you've heard the local rave music,
and seen the crazy Brummies that are slaves to it.
Arcadian lit up like an arcade treat,
where the shots are on offer, high heels on feet,
late teens and 20 somethings heading to Broad Street,
before you know it, you'll be 40, sipping red, red wine in Kings Heath.

Brum's the home of the canals
where I write poetry, and think,
the water's still, the only thing flowing is the ink.
I think of the horses pulling boats,
and know that Brum's engraved upon my soul,
like the walls holding scars of old ropes.
They'll never kill my love of Brum,
so if my passion is their target,
tell them bring a ring of bulls;
I bet you still couldn't mark it.
Like the shadow of the council house mountain,
or the fountain lying under,
Brum I promise,
I will stay around like the Rotunda.

I don't need ten letters; you know that ain't me,
you know I spell Birmingham, H-O-M-E.
So wherever I may be I will carry your thoughts with me.
        Forever yours,
            Mr I'm-in-love-with-my-city.

Predisposition

As a kid I watched the Olympics,
one gunshot started a race.
Eight black men running.
As a child, I asked my dad
why are they all black?
Apparently being born black, is being born
with a predisposition to be fast.

I like the sound of this!

As a man I sit at home and watch the news.
One gun shot, fired by a police officer, one black man dead.
The news shows a selection of others killed by the police.
My nephew asks me *why are they all black?*
Apparently being born black, is being born
with a predisposition to hold a lower value in society.

Apparently being born black, is being born
with a predisposition to be prejudicially treated
by a judicial system which is preordained
to be prejudice against you.

I don't like the sound of this.

To be honest, when I weigh up the pros and cons
I'd give the speed and the bullets back together.

Even the fastest man can't outrun a bullet.

One gunshot can start a race,
one gunshot can start a race riot,
one gunshot can end a life.

Waiting at Bloomsbury Park

If you had ever made it to Bloomsbury Park
like you told me you would,
we could have created magic.
Not Harry Potter, Diagon Alley magic,
not Chronicles of Narnia wardrobes,
lions, rings and trees magic.
Real magic.

We would swing on monkey bars,
swing over the deepest canyon,
desperate to never know if the rumours
about falling off were true.
We would fly in the helicopter
from the park to The Carriage,
ride in The Carriage to the swings
and swing until we sat just above
the horizon, just below heaven.

We would have lost time,
lost inhibitions in our exhibition,
lost the use of our sense,
to the use of our senses,
sensibility overthrown
by a sensory overload.
We would have made magic.

I think part of me is still waiting
at Bloomsbury Park.
Part of me always will be.

Thank you

Kerri Bailey, you have put up with me being eternally busy and equally crazy. You knew the boy Waiting at Bloomsbury Park, and you helped to build the man he is today! I love you.

Dad, you were my inspiration then and you are my inspiration now. When people say I'm just like you, they give me too much credit, and they do you an injustice.

Amerah Saleh, I could listen to you read poetry forever and never get bored. I could talk with you about poetry, life, Yemen, politics or anything, and I would be enhanced by the time shared. Thank you for being the superstar that you are.

Brum on Tour, you ladies have reinvigorated my love of poetry and given me a new-found love of road trips, snacks and childish laughter. Long may it continue.

Leon Priestnall, when I started to engage with the Birmingham poetry scene and with my own writing, you were a friend, you were an example and you were the legend that you still are today.

Mike Hayden and Lumi HD, your support of this project has been invaluable, I can't tell you how much I appreciate it.

Aaron Moses-Garvey, the way that you have supported this project, the way in which you conduct yourself and everything that you do reminds me what excellence looks like, I am proud of all that you do.

My brothers Shaun, Lucien, Dwayne, Nathaniel, Ayinde, Matthew, Darrell, Aaron and Daniel – We came up together, we have fell hard, but we always come back harder and stronger.

Anne Holloway, for Big White Shed, for this book, for all of it.